Round Tower Churches in Mid Norfolk, North Norfolk and Suffolk

A series of detailed day tours

Foreword by
The Right Rev'd Graham James
Lord Bishop of Norwich

Text and photographs by Jack Sterry

Acknowledgements

Once again I would like to express my appreciation to family and friends who have encouraged me in writing this book and the ones that have gone before.

I would like to say a special thank you to the Lord Bishop of Norwich, the Rt. Revd. Graham James, who also wrote the Foreword of my second book, *Round Tower Churches on the Norfolk and Suffolk Border*, and kindly agreed to write the Foreword to this book. I am extremely grateful to him as I know that he is a very busy man. The Foreword is excellent as it reminds us not only of the structure and beauty of the churches but also the reason for their very origin.

As I have mentioned before, I am a computer illiterate, and I am afraid I show little interest in changing! In view of this I am particularly grateful to Pam Paterson for the great help she has given me in the typing and setting out of the many drafts I have prepared, not only for this book but also on the earlier editions. I would also like to thank Allan, her husband, for his help in dealing with the various maps to show the locations of the churches.

I am very grateful to Richard Barham, Treasurer of the Round Tower Churches Society, for pointing me in the right direction in the drafts on my last couple of books. He certainly stopped me making a few silly mistakes! To my old school friend, Vic Hopes, and to Rosemary, a constant friend, a sincere thank you for all the great help and encouragement they have given me. All of this is very much appreciated.

As this may possibly be my last book, I would like to say a particular thank you to Mike Dawson, Steven Pyke and other colleagues at Crowes, my printers, for their excellent presentation of all my books. Without their expertise I do not think I would have sold anywhere near as many books.

First published 2010
© Jack Sterry 2010
Published by Jack Sterry
Sleepy Hollow 1A De Montford Road Kenilworth CV8 1DF

ISBN 0-9544948-4-9

Printed and bound by Crowes Complete Print, Norwich

Contents

THE BISHOP OF NORWICH
Bishop's House
Norwich

Foreword

by the Lord Bishop of Norwich

Jack Sterry's enthusiasm for round tower churches finds further expression in this book. It is infectious. His own fascination with these churches kindles our own too.

There are various theories to explain the numbers of round tower churches in East Anglia. While this book adds further to the literature about them, its best quality is that it communicates something of the spirit which inhabits these ancient places of worship. Within them we feel a deep connection with our ancestors whose faith and imagination built them in such a way that they have endured to the present day. In our own generation we treasure them by inhabiting them and worshipping in them. By doing so we are refreshed by the same stream of living water flowing down the centuries. That living water finds its origin in Jesus Christ, without whom no church of any description would be built at all.

So these churches can be enjoyed and cherished at many different levels. The sales of these books have benefitted many other churches through Jack Sterry's generosity. We are very grateful to him.

The Rt. Revd. Graham James
Lord Bishop of Norwich

Introduction

In the Introduction of my last book, *Round Tower Churches to the East, West and South of Norwich*, I said that I thought it would probably be my last book. However, on looking through some of my papers I found I had details of about eight churches almost completed. I had not used them before as they did not fit in with the earlier books. I decided it would be a waste not to use them and here I am again!

As I have mentioned in my earlier books, I grew up in Gloucester and Norwich and went to the City of Norwich School during the war years, 1939–1944. I then joined the Norwich Union, firstly at Head Office and then to Leeds Branch. In about 1956 I made the move into Insurance Broking and I was variously based in Leeds, Manchester, Dublin, Nottingham and Sheffield and lastly to Birmingham. During these times I luckily visited Norfolk fairly regularly, both on business and on holiday.

When I was in Norwich as a youngster, we had no round tower churches near to us at home and I must admit I didn't even know they existed. Once retirement came, my visits to Norfolk increased considerably. During one of my visits to North Norfolk I was driving from Wells-next-the-Sea to Hunstanton and noticed a church on a hill which was at Burnham Norton. Continuing along the main road I then came to Burnham Deepdale and then to Titchwell. The churches in these locations were all very different but they all had round towers. At Burnham Norton St. Margaret's Church, I was very impressed with the beautiful Jacobean pulpit and the very 'strong' Norman font. Then to Burnham Deepdale St. Mary's Church, which I have always considered to be one of my favourite churches – there was the magnificent calendar font. In fact I became 'hooked' on these churches and became a member of the Round Tower Churches Society which I strongly recommend to others who show any similar interest. I also bought an excellent book, which I understand is now out of print, by the late W. J. Goode, *Round Tower Churches of South East England*, which has virtually been my guide to visit many churches.

There are some 130 round tower churches remaining in Norfolk today, together with the ruins of several others. There are also 42 in Suffolk and a few others in Essex, Cambridgeshire, Sussex and Berkshire. I believe in total there are approximately 180 round tower churches in the United Kingdom.

About eight or nine years ago (I had been photographing the churches for some years) I began to realise that most of the books on round tower churches were very 'black and white' and in great detail, which to the casual reader was maybe rather too much. I had never written a book before but in business I had to write quite a number of long articles so that gave me a bit of experience and background. I decided with my books I would try to be different with a lot of colour photographs, and to divide the books into tours. I hoped these tours could easily be managed by people even on holiday, when maybe they had a damp morning and didn't know what to do with their time.

I am not an historian and I wasn't trying to be an 'expert', I was trying to encourage people who normally wouldn't visit these churches, to do so. The books seem to have been quite successful as, excluding this new book, I've sold well over four and a half thousand. I've also been able to donate approximately £13,000 to the church charities, i.e. The Norfolk and Suffolk Churches Trusts and The Round Tower Church Society.

Whilst the ages of these churches are important, more to some than to others, I think we should try to enjoy these churches more for what they are – beautiful examples of buildings which have lasted, in the majority of cases, for well over a thousand years. We should also remember what the Lord Bishop of Norwich said in his excellent Foreword, that is to try to remember the reason for their very existence and not argue so much about the question of age. We are very lucky to have these wonderful buildings still remaining in East Anglia.

There are many theories as to why round towers. It is interesting to know there are round tower churches in various parts of Europe but no more in the United Kingdom except in basically East Anglia. With regard to Norfolk and Suffolk, a large number of historians feel that the reason for round towers in these churches was because at the time of the building there was a lack of large stone in the area, but a predominance of flint which could be used easily to build round tower churches. There were also other local stones that were used in the building of some of these churches, such as conglomerate, known as pudding stone, and carstone which is a north west Norfolk stone known as gingerbread stone. One particular church detailed in this book that shows the use of conglomerate is St. Lawrence at Beeston St. Lawrence, where the additional stone was used considerably in the lower part of the tower. There are various schools of thought as to why 'round towers'. Some feel that the origin came from instructions that were possibly sent out by King Atherstan, formerly Guthrum, a Viking leader who had settled in the Norfolk area. King Atherstan, was said to have been based at the Saxon cathedral in North Elmham, Norfolk.

I have thoroughly enjoyed writing my four books on round tower churches in the last ten years or so and I have found it extremely interesting and educational. This book may possibly be my last as I am unfortunately not based in Norfolk or Suffolk but live in the Midlands and I am finding it more difficult to do the required research from a distance, and unfortunately I also suffer from lack of mobility.

Thank you all for your very kind support, and who knows, I may try something similar in the future.

Suggested Tours from Norwich

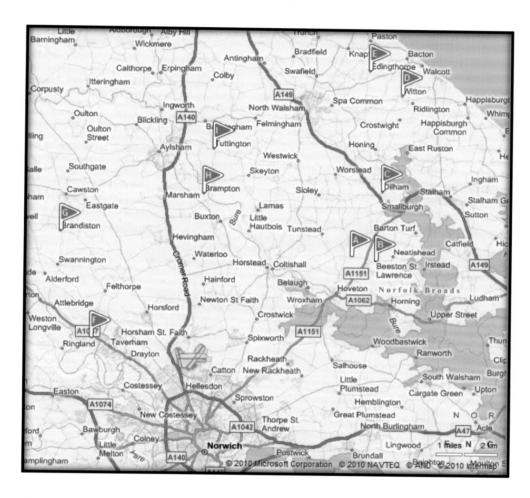

Tour 1 – From Norwich

A. Ashmanhaugh – St. Swithin's
B. Beeston St. Lawrence – St. Lawrence
C. Dilham – St. Nicholas
D. Witton – St. Margaret's
E. Edingthorpe – All Saints

Tour 2 – From Norwich

F. Taverham – St. Edmund's
G. Brandiston – St. Nicholas
H. Brampton – St. Peter's
I. Tuttington – St. Peter and St. Paul's

Tour 1: from Norwich

Ashmanhaugh – St. Swithin's Church
Beeston St. Lawrence – St. Lawrence Church
Dilham – St. Nicholas Church
Witton – St. Margaret's Church
Edingthorpe – All Saints Church

Leave Norwich on the A1151 to and through Wroxham. Continue on the same road for about three miles turning to Ashmanhough on your left. Continue down that road for about three quarters of a mile to the turning on the right leading up to St. Swithin's Church. The church is set back on the left hand side about a quarter of a mile off the byroad mentioned above.

Return to the A1151, turn left and after approximately half a mile you will find the church of St. Lawrence, Beeston St. Lawrence on the right hand side of the road.

On leaving Beeston St. Lawrence, continue on the A1151 to the A149 on the left hand side of the road. Turn down the A149 and in approximately one mile on the right hand side of the road, there is a signpost to Dilham. St. Nicholas Church is situate about half a mile from the main A149.

Continue on the A149 towards North Walsham. After approximately a mile and a half, take the right turn to Honing and continue through to Witton – I had great difficulty finding the church at Witton until I was advised to take the Witton to Bacton road. St. Margaret's Church is set back on the right hand side of the road after approximately a mile or so.

After leaving the church, continue on the road to Bacton. In Bacton turn left on the main road and after about half a mile or less there is a turn on the left hand side to Edingthorpe. Continue on this road until you meet Edingthorpe village and set back, about half a mile, in a field, on the right hand side, is All Saints Church.

St. Swithin's Church
Ashmanhaugh, Norfolk

The church (figure 1) consists of a round tower, nave, chancel and south porch. There was originally a vestry on the north side but this has been demolished. The round tower is the smallest in Norfolk having an internal diameter of just six feet. There has been quite a lot of restorations and repairs – the tower was rebuilt and the fabric of the church repaired in 1849 and there have been further restorations in 1867 and again more recently in 1921.

Figure 2 shows the north wall with the now blocked north door, inside which is an Early English pointed arch within an earlier Norman arch (figure 5). The Norman arch does not appear in figure 2.

Entering the church by the south porch which is constructed of knapped flint, are the partial remains of a holy water stoup (figure 3). On entering the church proper, to the left is the Victorian font with a round bowl and octagonal stem and base (figure 4).

Figure 2

Figure 3

Figure 5 shows the blocked up northern doorway and the evidence of the Early English pointed arch below an earlier Norman arch.

One of the older benches at the back of the nave (figures 6a and 6b) have carvings of a lion and a dragon on the bench end. Opposite, at the back of the benches, on the south side are carved panels depicting the five wounds Christ suffered on the cross and the date 1531.

Figure 7 shows the church from halfway down the nave towards the chancel. Most of the furniture including the pulpit is of Victorian (1840s) period. There is a piscina in the south-east end of the nave denoting that before the Reformation there was a side altar.

Figure 7 also shows the chancel and the east window, shown more clearly in figure 7a. The glass is signed by William Morris and Company of London and dates to 1929. The brass plate on the altar step tells us that the glass was erected in memory of the Reverend Walter Cubison, who was vicar of the church from 1917 to 1928.

Figure 8 shows the communion rail, the altar, and the remains of the piscina and sedilia. It also shows, cramped in the corner between the nave and the piscina, the tomb of Honour Black Bacon, who died in 1597 aged 17. Honour is said to have died on the eve of her wedding and the epitaph, which is partly illegible, says "A better mayden lived not then and now her like doth lack". The coat of arms includes the three pigs of the bacon family.

Figure 4

Figure 5

Figure 7

Figure 8

Figure 6a

Figure 6b

Figure 7a

St. Lawrence Church
Beeston St. Lawrence, Norfolk

The church is situated close to the main road (A1151) between Wroxham and Stalham. Figure 1 shows the church consisting of round tower, nave open to the chancel (as shown in figure 5) and porch. Figure 2 shows the north side of the church. At the western end of the nave wall may be seen the outline of a smaller Saxon nave.

The round tower is mainly flint built but with a good deal of conglomerate in the lower part of the tower (early 12th century). The upper part of the tower is thought to be late 12th century. In 1945 a V2 rocket caused damage to a good deal of the late 18th century stained glass in various parts of the church. The tower parapet was not actually destroyed by the rocket – but was removed for safety reasons. (Health and Safety!) The nave was rebuilt in the early 14th century and the chancel shortly afterwards. The porch was built in 1803.

Figure 2

Figure 3

Inside the base of the tower (figure 3) is a wooden board which used to stand by the entrance to the churchyard as seen in many earlier photographs of the church. The board is self explanatory and most historians now agree that the date of the tower is Saxon.

Figure 4 shows the carved stone font believed to date from the 1803 restoration. Figure 5 shows the church from the tower arch looking toward the chancel and the 19th century east window. Shown in the nave are the Victorian benches, some of which have beautiful end carvings (figure 5a). Also in the nave is the pulpit (figure 6), also believed to be Victorian.

In the chancel is the organ (figure 7) rebuilt by E.W. Norman of Norwich – the organ incidentally hides one of the memorials to the Preston family.

In the south-east corner of the chancel is the rather battered remains of a piscina which must have been very grand when it was still in use (figure 8). The chancel is full of memorials and slabs to the Preston family (earlier spelt Prefton). There is a very wide selection of memorials and to illustrate a few I have tried to create a montage from some of the earliest ones to some of the more recent (figure 9). These memorials are very interesting and date from when the Preston's acquired the estate in 1640 from the Hobarts of Blickling Hall. The Preston Arms are ermine tails with three crescents on the band above.

Figure 4

Figure 5

Some of the memorials not only include the Preston Coat of Arms but also those of other members of the family who married into the Preston family.

Figure 7

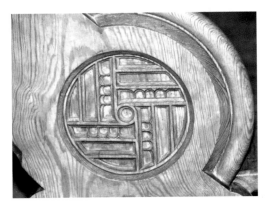

Figure 5a

Figure 6

Figure 8

Here Lyeth ye body of Iane Preston
5th daughter of Isaack Preston Esqr
by Elizabeth his wife who departed
this life ye 9th day of August 1694
Ætatis Suæ 12°

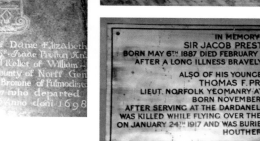

Here Lyeth the Body of Dame Elizabeth
Preston, second wife of Sr Isaac Preston Knt
who was the Widdow and Relict of William
Worts of Trunch in ye County of Norff Gen
And Daughter of Riches Browne of Fulmodiston
in the Said County Esqr who departed
this life August the 24 Anno doni 1698

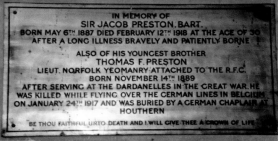

IN MEMORY OF
SIR JACOB PRESTON. BART.
BORN MAY 6TH 1887 DIED FEBRUARY 12TH 1918 AT THE AGE OF 30
AFTER A LONG ILLNESS BRAVELY AND PATIENTLY BORNE

ALSO OF HIS YOUNGEST BROTHER
THOMAS F. PRESTON
LIEUT. NORFOLK YEOMANRY ATTACHED TO THE R.F.C.
BORN NOVEMBER 14TH 1889
AFTER SERVING AT THE DARDANELLES IN THE GREAT WAR. HE
WAS KILLED WHILE FLYING OVER THE GERMAN LINES IN BELGIUM
ON JANUARY 24TH 1917 AND WAS BURIED BY A GERMAN CHAPLAIN AT
HOUTHEM

"BE THOU FAITHFUL UNTO DEATH AND I WILL GIVE THEE A CROWN OF LIFE"

Sir EDWARD
HULTON PRESTON
D.S.O. M.C.
5th BARONET
OF BEESTON HALL
NORFOLK
Born 17th September 1888
Died 7th December 1963
Blessed are the pure
in heart

IN
MEMORY OF
SIR THOMAS PRESTON
SIXTH BARONET O.B.E.
PROSPECTOR DIPLOMAT
AND MUSICIAN
BORN 1886 DIED 1976
AND HIS WIFE
ELLA HENRIETTA
1888–1989

Figure 9

St. Nicholas Church Dilham, Norfolk

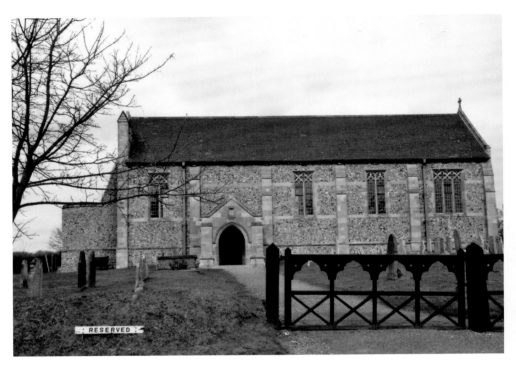

This church is very unusual, certainly to someone who had not seen it before. It is a very large church in a quiet area, and even more surprising, as most round tower churches are hundreds of years old, and one comes across a very handsome church (figure 1) that was fully restored in 1931 on exactly the same ground as the ancient Dilham church stood.

The church has a very interesting history. During the 18th century a square towered church virtually collapsed. In 1775 an attempt was made to restore the nave without success and in 1835 was so badly cracked it had to be pulled down and was replaced by an entirely round towered church. This round tower only lasted about 70 years and in 1931 it was reduced and is now the ground floor baptistry.

Figure 2

The 1931 restoration was the result of Henry Morse Taylor of Dilham Hall bequeathing money to build the church. It was designed by the architect C.G. Hare and with local North Walsham builders, Cornish and Gaymer. The church is certainly a splendid building and much taller than most round tower churches.

Figure 3

On entering the church, is an imposing war memorial on the north wall, depicting six men from the village who were killed in the 1914–18 war and another five in the 1939–45 war (figure 2).

The church is one single entity between the nave and the chancel and I understand it was the same in the earlier church. Figure 3 shows toward the three panelled east window, the altar and the imposing organ. Figure 3 also shows briefly the excellent hammer beam roof, shown in greater detail in figure 4, and beautiful wooden angels with outspread wings – shown more clearly in figure 5.

Turning to the east end of the church, as mentioned before, the round tower has been turned into a baptistry with the font which is partly Medieval and partly restored (figure 6). It is said that the top four inches are new. The bowl to the font is eight sided, on each side there are three blank arches with quatrefoils below.

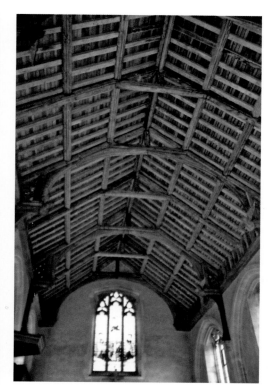

Over the tower arch are the Royal Arms of George III (1760–1820) (figure 7). These Arms were before 1801 when the Royal Arms were altered with the Act of the Union with Ireland.

Figure 8 shows one of the legislabs from the old church that have been relaid in the centre aisle. Figure 8 shows the slab in respect of Richard Paul who died in 1739 aged 33 years and several other members of his family.

The new church is fairly lofty. The north and south windows are plain but inside the arches are very attractive. The walls have all been inlaid with flint, part of which came from the old church.

Figure 4

Figure 5

Figure 6

Figure 7

Figure 8

St. Margaret's Church
Witton, Norfolk

Witton is a well spread out village, two or three miles from the coast and about three miles from Bacton, on the north Norfolk coast. Witton was first mentioned in the Domesday Book as Wittuna and I'll mention this further, later in the book.

This large church (figure 1) is in a very isolated position and comprises a round tower, nave, chancel, south aisle and porch. The north and west walls of the nave are said to be the earliest part of the church and are thought to date from the late Saxon period. There is considerable use of conglomerate, an iron bound stone which is a feature of many late Saxon churches particularly in north Norfolk.

There are two round double splayed windows on the north side of the nave, believed to be Saxon. The round tower is thought to be later than early parts of

Figure 2

Figure 3

the nave, although the base of the tower is thought to date from the late Saxon period, although the rest of the structure including the belfry, is later.

The chancel was added in the 13th century, the south aisle early in the 14th century and clerestory windows were added on both sides of the nave, after that period but the north aisle was never built. The windows in the south aisle date from the 19th century but are thought to be earlier copies of the originals. Figure 2 shows the font, believed to be 14th century with quatrefoils on each face of the bowl and trefoils on the arches to the stem. The font stands on a sold octagonal base.

Figure 3 shows the interior of the church looking through the chancel arch toward the east window, which is shown in greater detail in figure 4. The glass in this window is mid-Victorian. Figure 3 shows the arches and pillars to the south aisle and the clerestory windows above both the north and south walls. Figure 3 also shows the Victorian pulpit, also shown more clearly in figure 5.

In the chancel (figure 6) there is a fine example of a two seat sedillia showing dog tooth edging (Early English period) of the canopy. Nearby is a small piscina.

In the south aisle there are four box pews (figure 7) believed to be 18th century. On the south-east corner of the aisle, seen beyond the pews, is another piscina.

Figure 8 shows the organ which came from Witton Hall and now blocks the tower arch. The organ has a 'barrel organ' component comprising two barrels each with 10 tunes. Figure 8 also shows the old north entrance which is now blocked up.

On the floor of the sanctuary there are several brass plates marking 17th century graves. One of these is in respect of Thomas Parmenter and his wife who were married for 47 years, one dying in 1631 and the other 1627.

Figure 4

Figure 5   Figure 6

Figure 7   Figure 8

All Saints Church
Edingthorpe, Norfolk

Siegfried Sassoon, in an extract from his *The Old Sentry and Seven More Years*, describes this church: "It has a special dignity and simplicity, as though it were the faithful servant of the life around it." A lovely introduction for any church.

All Saints is in quite an isolated position, nearly half a mile away from the small Edingthorpe village. The church is on a slight rise and consists of a round west tower, nave, chancel and south porch. Edingthorpe is approximately two to three miles from Bacton on the north Norfolk coast.

Figure 1 shows the church in detail. The round tower is built of flint of varying sizes and a small amount of brick where repairs may have had to have been carried out. The tower is thought by many to be possibly late Saxon or early Norman, whilst others date it as post-

Figure 2

Figure 3

Norman. The octagonal belfry stage was added in approximately 1400. The belfry is flint built with brick quoins. Also shown are the nave, chancel and the 14th century porch which are all flint built. The nave has a thatched roof and the roofs of the chancel and the porch are both tiled. Figure 2 shows the tower in more detail (from the west). The small amount of 'patching up' in red brick is shown more clearly than in figure 1.

On entering the church through the south doorway the first point of interest is the 14th century font (figure 3). The font is octagonal in shape with quatrefoils on the bowl with a panelled stem. The font is set on two octagonal steps. Near to the font from the west wall is the organ which used to stand at the front of the nave where the reading desk now is. The organ said to be the work of Reverend G.P. Buck (1841–1919) is beside the small tower arch. Opposite the south door is a north doorway which is now blocked off and unusable.

Figure 4 taken from near the font, toward the east of church, shows the pews, many said to have been reconstructed from old box pews. Also shown are the east wall of the chancel, the rood screen and the pulpit which is on the south side of the church. On the north wall of the nave there are several 14th century paintings which were discovered under the plaster in 1937. Figure 5 is thought to show St. Christopher carrying the Christ Child on his shoulder. It is believed there may be other paintings under the plaster in various sections of the church.

Figure 6 shows the reading desk dated 1587 in the corner of the north wall and the wall to the chancel. The picture also shows a staircase to the now removed rood loft.

Figure 7 shows in more detail the pulpit dated 1632. There is a wrought iron stand for an hourglass attached to the pulpit. Nearby in the south-eastern corner of the nave is a piscina (figure 7a) believed to be 14th century. This can also be seen on the edge of the photograph figure 7. The piscina was used for washing Mass vessels which drained into the foundations so no holy waters left the church.

Figure 4

Figure 5

Figures 8a and 8b show the paintings on the rood screen which is said to be some of the best in Norfolk. There are very early original paintings dating back to the 14th century. From right to left (north to south) the pictures show in Figure 8a Bartholomew; St. Andrew; and St. Peter. Figure 8b shows St. Paul; St. John (or St. Catherine); and St. James the Great. There are some small holes in the screen which may possibly have been made by bullets fired by Cromwell's men! The stairs to the pulpit can be seen on the bottom corner of figure 8b.

On going into the chancel via the 14th century arch, on the southern wall is a modern metal sculpture (figure 9) said to have been made and presented by pupils from North Walsham High School – a great example of modern and ancient! In the chancel there are some very interesting floor memorials. Figure 10 shows one in respect of William Call who died in 1683. There is a very interesting mixture of windows throughout the church predominantly of the Decorated and Perpendicular periods – between 1250 and 1500.

The entrance to the church grounds is by the Lych gate erected by the Reverend Harvey Muriel who was rector from 1905 to 1925. The gate was erected as a memorial to his son who lost his life in 1915 in the Mediterranean and to all other parishioners killed during the Great War.

Figure 6

Figure 7

Figure 7a

Figure 8a

Figure 8b

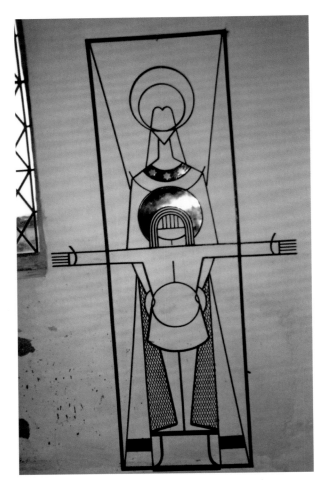

Figure 9

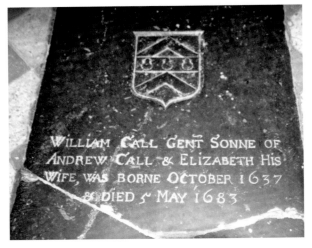

Figure 10

Tour 2: from Norwich

Taverham – St. Edmund's Church
Brandiston – St. Nicholas Church
Brampton – St. Peter's Church
Tuttington – St. Peter and St. Paul's Church

Leave the centre of Norwich on the A1067 towards Fakenham. After approximately three miles you will reach the village of Taverham where you turn left towards St. Edmund's Church, approximately three quarters of a mile from the main road.

Return to the A1067, turn left and after approximately two and a half miles at Attlebridge, turn right towards Brandiston, approximately three miles.

After leaving St. Nicholas Church, Brandiston, continue towards Eastgate, turn right and cross the B1149 towards Marsham and Brampton. St. Peter's Church is on the outskirts of the village of Brampton.

To Tuttington you could either a) return to the A140 towards Aylsham and two miles beyond Aylsham turn right to Tuttington village, or b) continue from Brampton through Burgh-next-Aylsham on a country road to Tuttington. St. Peter and St. Paul's Church is on the outskirts of the village on the right hand side of the road from Brampton.

St. Edmund's Church
Taverham, Norfolk

This very attractive church (figure 1) stands close to the north bank of the River Wensum and now consists of a round tower, chancel, nave, south aisle and porch. The origin of the church is thought to be overlapping Saxon and Norman times, and has undergone various additions and extensions over the years, with quite a lot of updating internally during the Victorian period.

The church is mainly flint built with a tiled and part slate roof. The octagonal belfry to the tower was added in the 15th century. The north and west walls of the nave are probably the oldest part of the church, though being covered with cement or plaster rendering, it is difficult to tell. To the north of the 14th century chancel there was originally a guild chapel dedicated to St. Mary. The chapel was demolished in the 17th century and a huge family vault was built by Thomas Sotherton in 1765 (figure 2).

Figure 2

Figure 3

Figure 3 shows the priest's door on the south of the chancel wall. On entering the church near the west end of the south aisle is the 15th century font (figure 4) with a plain octagonal bowl, and empty shields on each panel. Below the panel are shown symbols of the four Evangelists and the stem (figure 4a) shows carvings of the Saints and their emblems – Agnes with a lamb; James the Less with fullers club; Anne and her daughter, the Virgin Mary; Margaret and dragon; Giles with a deer; Lambert in Chasuble; Edmund with an arrow; and Leonard with chain.

Nearby on the windowsill is a carved wheel head cross dating from Saxon times, which may have been used as part of a preaching cross before the church was built (figure 5).

Figure 6 shows the west end of the nave showing the small tower entranceway at ground floor level and an organ gallery constructed in 1981 to house the organ. Also shown is the fine timbering to the roof. The east window (figure 7) was erected by Reverend J. Micklethwait of Taverham Hall for his mother, Lady Charlotte, who died giving birth to her 13th child in 1830. The glass was made later in 1873 by O'Connor.

Figure 4

In the south-east corner of the chancel, the piscina (figure 8), possibly 14th century, retains some of its colouring with a blue arch within its stone arch. Part of the flowers were also tinted red. Nearby there is a dropped sill sedilia with parts of its canopy and two small arches.

The west window in the north nave wall contains some fine English glass made circa 1466. It shows in the centre position the Crucifixion with the Blessed Virgin Mary and St. John on either side (figure 9).

Figure 10 shows the Victorian pulpit, which is ornately built with some excellent carvings. Also in the nave are some interesting poppyheads to the pews, an example is shown in figure 11.

On the south wall of the aisle is the Rector's Board dating back from 1274 to the present day (figure 12). There is also an interesting memorial to the three sons of Thomas and Mary Woodger who died in their infancy, 1720 (figure 13).

Figure 4a

The communion rails show excellent pierced carving work. The rails are said to have come from a screen in Thurgarton church (which once had a round tower) in the 1850s.

Figure 5

Figure 6

Figure 7

Figure 8

Figure 9

Figure 10

Figure 11

Figure 12

Figure 13

St. Nicholas Church
Brandiston, Norfolk

This church, about 10 miles from Norwich, is in a rather isolated setting and now in the care of the Churches Conservation Trust, formerly known as the Redundant Churches Fund, which administers over 300 churches throughout England. St. Nicholas is entered from a drive shared with Church Farm.

The church (figure 1) consists of a round west tower with an octagonal top, nave, chancel, north aisle and south porch and is flint built with a pantiled roof. Part of the church was demolished in the 18th century. Some say the church, or at least the tower, was rebuilt in 1890 but looking at figure 2 it appears that the early part of the tower, up to about 20 feet, seems to be of its original construction, i.e. maybe Norman, 12th century, and the alterations appear above this level, particularly at the later octagonal belfry stage.

Figure 2

Figure 3

The church has been altered many times and now forms a rather peculiar plan design. The rebuilding of the nave appears to have been carried out during the 14th century and the windows on the south side together with the west window are of the Decorated Period. As shown in figures 1 and 2 one of these windows is 'five petalled', the other two are more Perpendicular. The east wall of the church, thought to be 18th century, is of brick and flint with two large buttresses supporting it. The porch, figure 3, is of the same period as the nave, i.e. 14th century and has a small niche containing a statue of the patron saint (figure 4), which is thought to have been carved in 1938.

The interior of the church is fairly light as the majority of the windows are plain glass, some pre-1800. Figure 5, however, shows one of the gloomiest corners of the church and the only windows here are stained glass. There are however fragments of medieval glass in some of the south windows. The organ shown in figure 5 on the north wall is believed to be early 19th century, as are the pews which have poppy-headed ends, believed to be imitation of the Medieval style. The pulpit (figure 6) is also of a similar period.

The font (figure 7), given in memory of Revd. Thomas Medlicott Brown, who was rector from 1885–92, has an octagonal bowl bearing various motifs, the bowl standing on five small colonettes. The oak cover is topped by a wrought iron decoration. It is believed there was an earlier font in the church dated 12th/13th century. There is a chest at the west end of the nave and is thought to be Jacobean.

St. Nicholas was declared redundant in June 1997 as the parish of Brandiston was united with the neighbouring parish of Booton. The church became vested in the Round Tower Churches Fund in 1981.

Figure 4

Figure 5

Figure 6

Figure 7

St. Peter's Church
Brampton, Norfolk

Brampton is about two and a half miles south-east of Aylsham. St. Peter's church is at the north end of the village with only a few houses nearby. The church consists of a round tower, nave with an added south aisle, chancel, vestry and a 14th century porch.

The oldest part of the church is said to be the nave and it is thought that the tower was added possibly in the 11th or 12th century. The rather unusual, fairly narrow and tall round tower can be seen clearly in figure 1. The tower is mainly flint built but with two prominent bands of conglomerate stone which both decorate and bind the flint work. The very tall octagonal top was added to the tower in the 15th century. This is mainly stone and brick built.

The south aisle was added to the nave possibly in the 14th century at the same time that the porch was built,

Figure 2

although the porch has been extensively rebuilt at a latter period. Figure 2 shows the octagonal font at the western end of the church. The font is fairly plain but attractive – the bowl is decorated with plain shields surrounded by roselike frames. At some time the font has been painted white which hides some of its original stonework.

Figure 3 shows the timber built pulpit at the north-east corner of the nave. Also shown are the stone stairs which lead to the now demolished rood loft. At the top of the picture and also shown more clearly in figure 4, is a Roman urn set on a bracket above the pulpit. The urn is thought to date back to somewhere between the first and third centuries AD and was found by an archaeological excavation in 1977. The Romans normally favoured the pagan tradition of cremation followed by burial of the ashes in an urn.

Figure 3

Figure 5 shows some of the Brampton brasses which are shown in more detail in figures 6 and 7. These brasses are set on the north wall of the chancel. Figure 5 shows John Brampton, who died in 1535, in armour together with his two wives, Tomasine and Anne, who both wear kennel headdresses. Figure 6 shows the two wives in greater detail. Figure 7 shows the Brampton's four daughters – there would have been a brass in respect of their five sons, but unfortunately this has been lost. Figure 8 shows a floor brass memorial in respect of Charles Brampton who died later in 1631.

In the south-east corner of the chancel is a further memorial in respect of Robert and Isabel Brampton with their prayers being carried on scrolls – Robert Brampton, who died in 1468 was the grandfather of John Brampton, detailed above (figure 5). The memorial to Robert Brampton was not engraved until 15 years after his death. Another excellent brass in the south-east corner is to Edward and Joan Brampton, who both died in 1622.

Figure 4

Figure 5

Figure 7

Figure 6

Figure 8

St. Peter and St. Paul's Church
Tuttington, Norfolk

The village of Tuttington is situated on the eastern side of the A140 approximately 3–4 miles north of Aylsham. The lovely church is very close to the roadside on the far side of the village. The parish is mentioned in the Domesday Book (please refer to the Appendix at the end of this book).

It is thought the flint built round tower (figure 1) was erected possibly just after the Norman Conquest of 1066. The present spire was built in 1750 to replace a taller one that had collapsed. The narrow brick red parapet was possibly added at the same time. The tower is the oldest part of the present building, the chancel being the next oldest part of the church dating back to the 1300s. A priest's door is on the south side. The nave was rebuilt in 1450 and restored again in the late 19th century. The windows in the church vary considerably. The belfry windows of the tower have wide tracery of

Figure 2

Figure 3

the early 1200s. The windows in the chancel are of the Decorated style and those in the rebuilt nave are mostly Perpendicular.

The porch (figure 2) on the south side of the church is two stories in height but the upper floor has been removed. Over the entrance is a small niche at second floor level, possibly to have housed a statue. Figure 3 shows the northern doorway which is now disused and 'bricked up' with flint of a later period.

On entering the church by the main door is a disused staircase which formerly led to the upper floor over the porch. Figure 3 shows the northern doorway which is now disused and bricked up with flint of a later period.

Figure 4 shows the 15th century font. The octagonal sides have shields which are plain. Underneath the bowl are alternatively four lions and four roses. The oak font cover is said to be dated 1638. The fairly modern organ is shown in figure 4 beyond the font.

Facing from the font towards the east window (figure 5), one can see the medieval pew ends, the pulpit, the arch to the chancel, the altar and the east window.

Figure 6 shows in more detail the oak built pulpit of 1635 with the wrought iron hourglass stand over. Also shown is the old doorway to the rood screen loft which has been demolished. On the south side of the church, high up, is a corbel with the stone face of a dragon (figure 7).

Within the chancel the altar is a Jacobean table dated 1632. To the right of the altar is a piscina (figure 8) showing an unusual side opening which led to a plain seat (sedilia). In front of the altar rail are various memorials to the Elwin family. One of these (figure 9) is in respect of an Anne Elwin which makes quite interesting reading.

Figure 4

The main feature of the nave which I've referred to earlier, are 14 beautiful carvings of medieval pew ends. Because of lack of space, I've only included three, figures 10a, 10b and 10c. Figure 10a shows a man beating a tabor or drum; 10b shows an elephant and castle; and 10c shows a dragon. These carvings are well worth inspection, as are the pew ends to the choir stalls in the chancel.

Figure 6

Figure 5

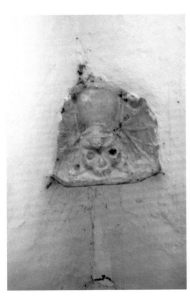

Figure 7   *Figure 8*

Figure 9

Figure 10a

Figure 10b

Figure 10c

Suggested Tour from Fakenham

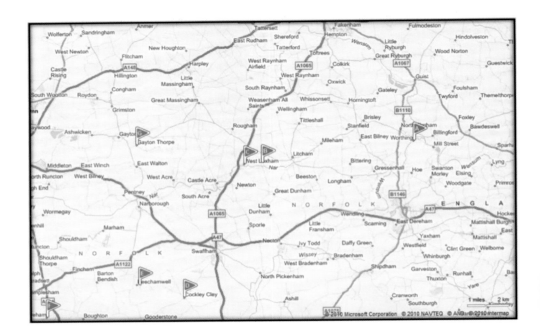

A. Worthing – St. Margaret's

B. East Lexham – St. Andrew's

C. West Lexham – St. Nicholas

D. Cockley Cley – All Saints

E. Beachamwell – St. Mary's

F. West Dereham – St. Andrew's

G. Gayton Thorpe – St. Mary's

This tour is quite long and could be divided into two: part a) starting from Fakenham to include Worthing and East and West Lexham, and part b) from Swaffham including the remainder of the tour.

Tour 3: from Fakenham

Worthing – St. Margaret's Church
East Lexham – St. Andrew's Church
West Lexham – St. Nicholas Church
Cockley Cley – All Saints Church
Beachamwell – St. Mary's Church
West Dereham – St. Andrew's Church
Gayton Thorpe – St. Mary's Church

From Fakenham take the A1067 to Norwich. After approximately five miles take the B1110 to North Elmham. After approximately three miles turn left on the B1145. After approximately one mile Worthing village is on your right hand side.

Returning to the B1145 turn left through North Elmham, Brisley, Mileham and Litcham. The Lexhams are on your left hand side, approximately two miles after Litcham. Turn left to East Lexham (St. Andrew's church is within a farmyard). Leave East Lexham and proceed up the hill about a mile to West Lexham. St. Nicholas Church is up a slope near a grassed triangle in the road.

Leave West Lexham church and continue to the A1065. Turn left towards Swaffham, approximately four miles. Go through Swaffham centre but as leaving, Cockley Cley is signposted on the right hand side of the road. Proceed down the country lane approximately four miles to Cockley Cley. All Saints church is on the far side of the village.

Proceed back to the centre of the village turning left to Beachamwell, approximately three miles. St. Mary's church is in the centre of the village.

Leaving Beachamwell on your left continue as to the A1122, but beforehand turn left marked to Barton Bendish. Carry on through that village through Broughton to Wareham. At the A134 turn right and after approximately a mile and a half turn left to West Dereham. St. Andrew's church is before the entrance to the village.

Return to the A134, turn left and at the junction with the A1122 turn right for approximately six miles and at the A47 turn left and after approximately three miles turn right onto the B1153 through East Walton to Gayton Thorpe. St. Mary's church is at the end of the village, approximately two and a half miles from the A47.

St. Margaret's Church
Worthing, Norfolk

The first time I visited this area I managed to find the small, attractive village but could find no trace of the church. In desperation I decided to follow a stony road up to a back entrance of Swanton Morley airfield only to be turned back by a 'No Entry' sign. On my return, much to my amazement, I found the church on the left hand side of the lane in what looked at first to be an overgrown field. Obviously it was the time of the year and on my second visit the whole area looked so much more attractive.

Worthing is only a few miles away from North Elmham where the early Bishops of East Anglia resided from the 8th century or earlier. St. Margaret's is a lovely and unusual little church. As you approach it from the east end, (figure 2), you realise that the church now consists of a nave, tower, and porch. There is no chancel, this having been demolished believed to be early in the 19th century. There are still a few remains of the chancel footings which show that it was a

Figure 2

Figure 3

little smaller in width than the nave. The east wall consists of a mixture of flint, stone debris, stone tiling, etc., but with no window. There is a small stone cross on the gable.

This is one of the churches where there is argument as to which came first, the tower or the nave. The tower, which is now one of the shortest of all round towers, being only 25 feet tall, is very old and the lower two thirds are believed by some to be Saxon, possibly 10th or early 11th century. The tower was reduced to its present size in the 18th century. Some historians believed that the church itself may be earlier, possibly late 9th and early 10th century. The tower is flint built with a small amount of early brick at belfry level. There are three belfry windows or bell openings. These are brick and timber lined with timber slats.

The nave, which also houses the sanctuary following the demolition of the chancel, is fairly simple with a three light Perpendicular window on both the south and north sides. The southern window is shown in figure 1. There is also a small bricked up doorway, believed to be Norman, on the north side of the nave. Figure 1 shows the south facing porch, believed to be 15th century. Inside the porch is the main but fairly simple, Norman doorway which has beautiful zig-zag stonework round the arch (figure 4).

Inside the nave there are several interesting items. On the east wall the remains of the old, very wide chancel arch can still be seen. On the north side of the east wall is a charming late Perpendicular niche, (figure 5) with an elaborate canopy over. This will possibly have housed a statue. The pulpit nearby is quite modern. On

Figure 4

the south side of the nave is a marble memorial in memory of Edwin George Neal which was erected in 1901 following his death by dysentery during the Boer War in September 1900 (figure 6).

In the south-west corner of the nave is a very striking and very interesting, but rather primitive, font (figure 7). This is made up of a brick plastered plinth supporting the base of a Norman or early-English font with circular corner shafts, the top portion and bowl are believed to be carved from an old churchyard cross. Nearby to the east of the doorway is a holy water stoup. The tower arch on the west wall is late Perpendicular in style.

Figure 5

Figure 6

Figure 7

St. Andrew's Church
East Lexham, Norfolk

Said by many historians to be possibly the oldest of the round tower churches in England, possibly dating back to the 9th century. This very interesting church is approached through a farmyard. The church stands on a small mound and is surrounded by a circular walled churchyard. It is thought to be the site of an early Pagan church before Christianity came to Norfolk in the 7th century. The church is one of several in the county that demonstrates the Christian victory over Paganism.

As can be seen from figure 2, the tower is quite crudely shaped, its stones having been laid in various layers with occasional bands or layers of larger flints. At belfry level the tower tapers inwards and contains three unusual Saxon type window openings, two of which are shown in figures 3a and 3b. Figure 3b is in the form of a finely cut Maltese Cross in a stone frame and may have been added in the Norman period.

Figure 2

Figure 3a

Figure 4 shows a lancet window at lower level and is said to have been added during the 14th century. The church walls are also thought to be from the Saxon period and run continuously through the nave to the chancel. As shown in figure 5 there is no chancel arch or rood screen. The rood screen may possibly have been demolished at the time of the Reformation, a time of 'restoration'. The windows are of the Perpendicular period.

Externally the walls of the church have been 'restored' with lime mortar and are in part painted with a plastic paint which is rather out of keeping.

The porch on the south of the church was built at a later date than the church, and contains a 12th century stone coffin lid on the floor. The opposite northern doorway has been blocked and the space filled in with a colourful war memorial (figure 6) which shows St. Michael driving out the devil in the form of a dragon.

On the west wall above the tower arch, are the Commandment Board and the royal arms of George IV. Between the south doorway and the former arch is a Victorian font, decorated with archways and flowers.

Figure 3b

Figure 4

On the south wall of the nave is a very fine door with decorative ironwork (figure 7). This leads to a book cupboard which is in the thickness of the south wall, and, earlier, contained stairs to the demolished rood loft.

In the chancel, the East window (figure 8) is of the Perpendicular period with fine stone tracery – the coloured glass is from about 1859, depicting amongst others, the Annunciation, the Nativity and the Crucifixion. The chancel also contains a beautiful angled piscina, from the 14th century Decorated period (figure 9).

Figure 5

Figure 6

Figure 7

Figure 8

Figure 9

St. Nicholas Church
West Lexham, Norfolk

The church (figure 1) stands on raised ground overlooking the small village and farms. The church has been partly restored during the last 200 years. The nave is said to have been completely rebuilt in 1881 when the roof was lifted – an earlier drawing of the church shows the nave and chancel all with one roof. This structural repair work to the nave appears to have been a gift from the Second Earl of Leicester who was the landowner – his tenant lived in the nearby Hall. Also in 1881 the chancel was restored, largely paid for by the rector, Reverend F.F. Reavely, in memory of his wife who laid the foundation stone three months before her death. There is a plaque commemorating this restoration in the chancel.

The church is mainly flint built and with a tiled roof. The tower is thought by some historians to date back to Saxon days of the 11th century, but it does not appear

Figure 2

Figure 3

to have any definite Saxon features. As shown in figure 2 the tower has been extensively repaired. In 1993, the tower had severe cracks and threatened to collapse, similar to the church at Cockley Cley. The church was strengthened with steel stitching in supports enclosing the tower, after which the whole surface was rendered. There are four belfry openings to the tower, believed to be 14th century, and are set diagonally (NE, SE, SW and NW – the south-west opening has been blocked up). Figure 2 shows the south-eastern opening.

Figure 3 shows the flint and tiled porch, possibly built at the same time as the alterations in the 19th century. The inner doorway (from the photograph) appears earlier than the restoration.

Entering the church from the main entrance, the font (figure 4) nearby has an early, possibly Norman, bowl which is supported by a modern stem. Near the font, in the south-west corner of the nave, is a cast iron tombstone which has been brought inside the church to protect it from the weather (figure 5). It commemorates John Jex, who died in 1874.

Turning internally to the east of the church (figure 6) is the chancel arch believed to be 14th century. Also seen is the lectern, the pulpit, the altar and the east window, shown more clearly in figure 7. The window is dated 1872 and is signed by L. Lobin of Tours, a French glazier. It shows Christ giving his blessing surrounded with scenes of the Nativity; the angel at the empty tomb; Christ's Presentation at the inner Temple; and the Supper at Emmaus and the Ascension.

Figure 4

Figure 8 shows an alms box on a pew end with an excellent carving of a donkey. This was given in memory of Geoffrey Palmer who was the estate carpenter and church warden from 1937 to 1967.

The church is tiled with tiles of three colours (black, white and red) which were paid for by the Second Earl of Leicester.

Figure 5

Figure 6

Figure 7

Figure 8

All Saints Church
Cockley Cley, Norfolk

Cockley Cley is approximately six miles south west of Swaffham. The church as it is today is shown in figure 1. It originally had a round tower until it fell down in August 1991. The remains of the tower are shown in figure 2 at the west end of the church. The remaining church consists of a nave with two aisles and a chancel.

There is an earlier church in Cockley Cley of Saxon origin dedicated to St. Mary. As with many of the round tower churches there are great arguments or discussions as to the ages of the structures. Some schools of thought date this church (All Saints) as Saxon, even early Saxon, whereas others date it as 14th century or slightly before. Some feel that the remains of the tower are possibly of the earlier period because of the thickness of the walls. I am not an historian and it is difficult to comment further.

Figure 2

Figure 3

Apart from the tower, most of the church was restored in 1866–1868. The porch (figure 1) is Victorian but the 14th century doorway is still retained. Entering the church, near the west wall is a stone font, original age not known (figure 3). There is a small brass plaque saying that the font was restored by the parishioners in 1866. The stem has four engaged columns and the eight sided bowl is decorated with a simple quatrefoil on each face. The wooden pulpit (figure 4) on a stone platform with steps is in the north-west corner of the nave. This like many items in the church dates from the Victorian restoration period.

In the south aisle there is a piscina (usually in the chancel) and also a stoup near the doorway (figure 5).

On entering the chancel, the first points of interest are the choir stalls which have poppyheads which are all different. The front stalls are for the smaller children. Figure 6 shows the communion rails and the table. The table had the upper carved wooden panels added in 1896. Also in figure 6 south of the altar (on the east wall) is an aumbrey – a cupboard used to store holy vessels. There are two further aumbreys on the north wall of the chancel.

Also in the chancel on the north wall is a very impressive memorial to Samuel Roberts who died aged 18 years in 1928 (figure 7). On the south wall of the chancel is a brass inscription (figure 8) in respect of John Dusgate who died in 1645. The shield shows three birds, possibly magpies, and the inscription also mentions his two sons and one daughter and their initials, ID, MD and WD.

On the floor of the chancel there are interesting memorials, several in respect of the Dashwood family who lived in the area in the 18th and early 19th centuries. Figure 9 shows one in respect of Elizabeth Dashwood, wife of John Richard Dashwood and their son Robert.

Figure 4

Figure 10 shows the memorial to Sir Peter Roberts, who died in 1985. Peter was the younger brother of Samuel (detailed above) who died in 1928. There is also a small memorial in respect of Sir Peter's wife, Lady Roberts, who died in 1998.

Figure 5

Figure 6

Figure 7

Figure 8

Figure 9

Figure 10

St. Mary's Church
Beachamwell (Beechamwell), Norfolk

The village is situated about five miles from the market town of Swaffham and some dozen or so miles to the Fens in the west and Brecklands in the south. The ancient earthwork known as Devils Dyke passes through the parish. Beechamwell is mentioned under various names in the Domesday Book: Becheswella; Bicham; Bycham; and Hekeswella. I understand the spelling Bycham was still used until 1568. At an annual parish meeting in 1977 it was voted for the spelling of Beachamwell to be the official spelling. This name is not however included in the index of the Domesday Book and may cause a little confusion. The area of the parish now know as Beachamwell was originally served by three churches, St. Mary's (figure 1), All Saints and St. John's. St. John's became redundant in 1558 and All Saints much neglected from the end of the 17th century.

Figure 2

Figure 3

It is thought by many historians, but not all, that the basic round tower of St. Mary's and parts of the nave were built in the Saxon period. Early English additions include the chancel and south aisle in 1340. The south aisle was extended and the north porch restored in 1832. The lower circular sections of the tower were built in two stages (figure 2). The upper portion showing two double Saxon window openings, those on the west and north being triangular and those on the south and east having semi-circular heads. In the 14th century, the octagonal belfry section was added. The tower is capped by a lead roof.

The roof of the nave and chancel has retained their medieval styled thatching. The south aisle was added in the 14th century. The north porch, as mentioned above, was possibly added in the 15th century and restored in the 19th century when other major restorations were carried out to the church. Internally, the tower arch is round headed (figure 3) with a distinctive door opening over.

As can be seen in figure 4, the ceiling of the nave and chancel are plastered to one single level. The nave is divided from the south aisle by a four bay arcade. The western bays are believed to date from 1340 but the two eastern bays were added in 1832 as part of a further extension. There is a piscina in the southern wall of the aisle (figure 5) which now contains the bust believed to be of St. Mary, which was a gift to the church.

The older woodwork in the building, includes the reading desk and the 17th century Jacobean pulpit, which are thought to have been originally combined as a two-decker pulpit, which were popular in the area (figure 6). The majority of the seating in the church dates to 1910. The church flooring is mainly made up of hexagonal tiles which were made locally and can be seen in figure 7 together with the slim, fairly modern pulpit. Figure 8 shows a floor slab in the central gangway marked OS and it may indicate the presence of a vault below. A clock was presented to the church in 1924 which is shown externally on the north wall of the tower.

Figure 4

Figure 5

Figure 6

Figure 7

Figure 8

St. Andrew's Church
West Dereham, Norfolk

West Dereham, which should not be confused with East Dereham (nearer to Norwich) is situated on the west of the county not far off the A134 Kings Lynn to Thetford road.

The village of West Dereham dates back to mid-Saxon times and it shows signs of Christianity back to the 7th century. There is said to have been a much smaller Saxon church of St. Peter's which has now vanished and the existing church was first recorded in 1246 although parts of it may date back to the late Saxon period. This quite unusual church stands on raised ground away from the present village, and like so many other Norfolk churches this may relate back to the plague or general movements of population.

The church, particularly the tower, is largely built of ironstone conglomerate (compressed gravel and small

Figure 2

Figure 3

pebbles) – I understand this stone is still found locally. The church, particularly the tower, (figure 2) has a heavy solid Norman appearance. The tower is somewhat larger (23 feet in external diameter at the base) than most churches of this style and period. The octagonal belfry was added in the 16th century.

The church is largely original and all the church windows are of the Perpendicular period. The porch is 15th century with an later 17th gable. The door to the porch is 14th century. Near the door is a stoop (figure 3) set into the wall.

Internally, the nave and the chancel, which is also very wide, are separated by a wall with a very impressive archway (figure 4).

In the nave is an impressive Jacobean pulpit (figure 5) and reading desk (figure 6), possibly of the same period. The 14th century font (figure 7) is simple but still impressive.

There are several interesting memorials, the most impressive being the statue of The Honourable Colonel Edmund Soame, resplendent in his armour, (figure 8) who died in 1706. This monument is said to be one of the best in Norfolk. The heraldic monument to Thomas Dereham was made in Italy and erected in the church in 1722. (Although he did not die until 1728!)

Most of the church furniture is 17th century. Near the entrance at the west end of the church is a wooden turned poor box which is slightly dilapidated but also has an interesting quotation over (figure 9) and below.

"Be merciful after thy power
If thou has much give plentifully,
If thou has too little do thy diligence
gladly to give of that little
for so gatherest thyself a good reward in
the day of necessity."

Figure 4

In the tower room there is a bier dated 1683 and has carved names of R. Stafford and R. Coop (presumably church wardens at the time). The bier has unusual foldaway handles. Most of the windows have plain glass except for fragments of early glass in the east window and the south window of the nave. The fragments came from East Dereham Abbey when that was suppressed.

At the west of the churchyard is a very interesting gravestone (figure 10). Emmanuel Gaminara who died aged 98 in 1892. He was a soldier in the Second Imperial Guard under the great Napoleon and was thought to be the last survivor of the Napoleon retreat from Moscow in 1812.

Figure 5

Figure 6

Figure 7

Figure 8

Figure 9

Figure 10

St. Mary's Church
Gayton Thorpe, Norfolk

This old and largely unspoilt church is set in a raised position at the end of a small village green (figure 1). There have been few alterations to the church over the years mainly because the area is sparsely populated.

As with many round tower churches, various historians and experts differ over the age of the church. Most feel that the nave and chancel are the earliest being mid-Saxon with the tower being late-Saxon or during the Saxo-Norman overlap.

The church consists of a round, or partly oval, west tower, nave, chancel, south porch and north vestry which now covers the former northern entrance to the church.

The tower is believed to be late Saxon to about 40 feet and built of local flint, carstone and some conglomerate

Figure 2

Figure 3

as can be seen in figure 2. Figure 2 also shows two double splayed windows on the west face of the tower. The lower is believed to be Saxon with the upper, smaller window being Norman. Both were blocked up for several years but have been subsequently reopened. The portion of the tower above 40 feet is believed to be Norman with the belfry windows of the mid-Norman period.

The nave and chancel are believed to be early to mid-Saxon and are possibly the earliest parts of the church. Figure 1 shows the early south walls with windows added at a later period, possibly 15th century. Figure 1 also clearly shows the south porch which is now the main entrance to the church. The vestry on the north side was added in 1900 at which time new pews were added and the east window to the chancel was reglazed.

Figure 3 shows the inside of the nave and chancel with the east window which is not centrally set in the eastern wall. Below the window is a Georgian wooden reredos. Figure 3 also clearly shows the early English chancel arch which is supported by corbels on each side which are believed to represent Sir John de Thorpe and his wife, Alice (figure 4).

On the south wall of the chancel, there is a small piscina in the corner and a rather unusual stone sedilia with stone armrests (figure 5).

At the west end of the nave there is a seven sacrament font of the mid-15th century. This type of font is found mainly in East Anglia (figure 6). Many of these fonts were defaced during the Reformation but although the faces on this font have been damaged and hidden from view, the clothing is quite clearly shown. The north-eastern section depicts the Baptism (figure 7).

Figure 4

The local village sign (figure 8) clearly shows the church and also depicts the local farming area.

Figure 5

Figure 6

Figure 7

Figure 8

Suggested Tour from Bury St. Edmunds

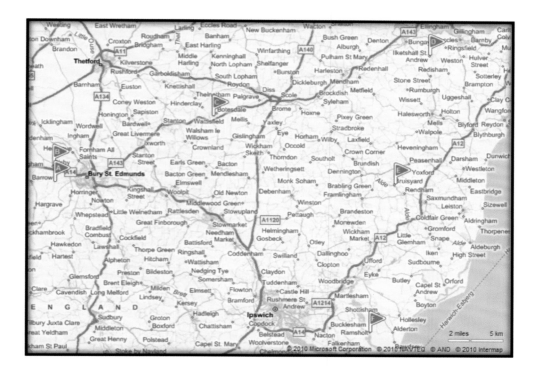

A. Little Saxham – St. Nicholas
B. Risby – St. Giles
C. Rickinghall – St. Mary the Virgin
D. Ilketshall – St. Margaret's

E. Bruisyard – St. Peter's
F. Ramsholt – All Saints

Tour 4: from Bury St. Edmunds

Little Saxham – St. Nicholas Church
Risby – St. Giles Church
Rickinghall – St. Mary the Virgin Church
Ilketshall – St. Margaret's Church

Leave Bury St. Edmunds on the A14 towards Newmarket. After approximately three miles at junction 41, turn left to Little Saxham. St. Nicholas church is on the edge of the village approximately a mile from the A14.

Return to the A14 and continue over to the other side of junction 41. Risby village is approximately a mile or so from the A14 and St Giles church is set off on a turning to your right. The church is on your left hand side in approximately three quarters of a mile.

Return to Bury St. Edmunds on the A14 and leave Bury St. Edmunds on the A143. After approximately ten miles Rickinghall village is on your left, Rickinghall Inferior is approximately a mile or so from the main road. St. Mary the Virgin church is set on your left hand side.

Return to the A143 and at approximately 13/14 miles there is a turning on your right down to Ilketshall. St. Margaret's church is on the far side of the village. Alternatively, you continue on the A143 to Bungay, turn right on the A144. Ilketshall village is approximately a mile and a half from the main road on your right hand side.

The other two Suffolk churches are not part of the tour but approximate details of how to locate them are as follows:

St. Peter's Church, Bruisyard: Take the A12 from Blythburgh running south. After approximately six miles turn right on the A1120 through Yoxford. After approximately five miles turn left on the B1120. After approximately three quarters of a mile turn left towards Bruisyard.

All Saints Church, Ramsholt: From Woodbridge take the B1083 towards Bawdsey. Pass Sutton Hoe National Trust premises, continue for approximately four miles. On your right hand side will be a signpost towards Ramsholt. Continue along that road until you find All Saints church on your left hand side. The church is in a lovely position, high up overlooking the River Deben.

St. Nicholas Church
Little Saxham, Suffolk

Little Saxham is a small village on the south side of the A14 (Junction 41), just to the west of Bury St. Edmunds. The church is in a corner situation on entering the village.

The tower is the earliest part of the church with the lower part probably Saxon and was maybe built for defence purposes against Danish raiders. Nikolaus Pevsner calls it, 'the most spectacular Norman round tower in Suffolk'. In the early 12th century the Normans added the belfry (figure 1).

On entering the church by the porch (also shown on figure 1), straight ahead is the rather plain font and the disused north door (figure 2). Standing by the door is a treble bell called Gabriel, cast soon after 1500. Turning to the right is the nave and the north aisle built in the early 14th century, in which the organ that came from

Figure 2

Figure 3

a redundant chapel in Downham Market was installed in this church in 1966 (figure 3). In all parts of the church are handsome bench-ends, mainly exotic animals. These are shown in figure 3 and figures 3a and 3b. Figure 4 shows the Jacobean pulpit restored in memory of the Reverend W.B. Hall (rector 1852–1885). Nearby is a beautiful carved oak eagle lectern which is given in memory of Kate Bayley who died in 1893 (figure 5).

On entering the chancel looking back into the nave (figure 6), one can clearly see the chancel arch and beyond it the tall tower arch and to the right the arcade of the north aisle. Turning towards the altar is a handsome communion rail (figure 7), coming forward in the middle in an elegant double curve. They were brought here from Little Livermore church in 1947. Also shown in the south-east corner is a piscina with a sedilia under the window. Over the altar is the east window, the stained glass having been made by Ernest Suffling in 1899 (figure 8). Also in the chancel there is a large memorial with a dedication: 'Cenotaph to Thomas Fitz Lucas of Little Saxham Hall, Solicitor General to King Henry VII, he died in London 7th July 1531, and was buried in London.'

Also in the chancel is a frieze at the side of the Lucas tomb. This was carved by Mrs Louise Cecilia Bazalgette Lucas Stratton, a direct descendant of Sir Thomas Lucas (figure 9). On leaving the church, on the left hand side of the porch, there are some unusual and somewhat eerie gravestones (figure 10).

Figure 3a

Figure 3b

Figure 4

Figure 7

Figure 5   Figure 6

Figure 8   Figure 10

Figure 9

St. Giles Church
Risby, Suffolk

Whereas St. Nicholas Church, Little Saxham, is on the south side of the A14 junction 41, St. Giles church, Risby, is off the same turning but on the north side of the road.

The settlement at Risby is one of five that can be traced back to the Danish Invasion of 865. Risby was also mentioned in the Domesday Book of 1086 which I will mention later.

Figure 1 shows the church with its Saxon/Norman round tower, which was thought to have been completed about the time of the Norman Conquest. A nave was added in the very early 13th century. The original chancel was demolished and a new one built in the mid-14th century. The south porch was added in the mid-15th century and the vestry erected in 1843.

Figure 2

On entering the church the first point of interest is the fine 15th century font. The bowl is carved with the symbols of the four Evangelists alternating with less common themes. The north-west and the south-west faces depict the Virgin Queen and the Arch Angel Gabriel respectively. The remaining two panels show a griffin and a pelican.

Nearby on the north wall are the remains of some fine wall paintings, although some have been partially destroyed by the insertion of windows, or later over-painting. The two paintings depicted are (figure 3a) the scene painted circa 1375 of Mary Magdalene anointing Christ's feet with ointment. The second, (figure 3b) shows a lancet window inserted circa 1275 with painted scrollwork and design. On the south wall opposite are the Royal Arms of George III painted at the end of the 18th century (figure 4).

Figure 3a

In both the nave and the chancel most of the benches are early Victorian although some earlier poppyheads remain, an example shown in figure 5. Also in the nave, figure 6 shows the pulpit (circa 1650) and the disused entrance to the rood loft.

The beautiful 15th century rood screen, (restored in 1966) is flanked by two niches either side, one on the north side contains a statue of St. Giles. (figures 6 and 6a).

Figure 8 shows the screen from the chancel side and also shows the decorative stonework of the chancel arch, which is Victorian re-use of Norman carved stones. Figure 9 looking toward the altar clearly shows the east window of the 14th century Decorated style. Also shown are the altar, the reredos and communion rails which were all carved by Reverend Samuel Alderson, rector 1839–1863. Shown more clearly in

Figure 3b

figure 9a are the piscina and sedilia in the south-east side of the chancel, together with a window of a similar style to the east window. Both windows contain fragments of glass of the 14th/15th century arranged by a rector's wife in the 19th century.

Figure 10 shows the priest's door leading into the chancel.

Figure 4

Figure 5

Figure 6

Figure 6a

Figure 7

Figure 7a

Figure 8

Figure 9

Figure 9a

Figure 10

St. Mary the Virgin Church
Rickinghall Inferior, Suffolk

The church is situated at the foot of a hill. There is a sister church at the top of the hill in Rickinghall Superior. It is thought the tower is Norman, but at that time the rest of the church was believed to have been wooden.

The beautiful church now consists of a tower, nave, chancel, south aisle and porch, as shown in figure 1. Figure 1 also shows the beautiful octagonal belfry, thought to have been added in the 14th century.

On entering the church figure 2 shows the octagonal font thought to be early 14th century with fine tracery patterns, as found in many of the windows.

Looking from the nave toward the chancel (figure 3) shows the chancel arch, the Holy table (17th century) and reredos (figure 4). The reredos, also shown more

Figure 2

Figure 3

clearly in figure 4a, is said to have been made by Victorian restorers when the rood screen was pulled down, seven of its panels being made into the reredos and repainted. Also in figure 4 is the east window decorated with Victorian glass. The rails to the sanctuary are also Victorian. On the south side of the sanctuary there is a piscina and a drop window sill sedilia (figure 5). Above the sedilia are two windows containing pieces of beautiful Medieval glass forming a framework to the windows. Figure 5 also shows the end of the sanctuary wall.

The south aisle has four imposing bays, the pillars showing the heads of an Abbot, a King and a Queen, possibly Edward II and his wife, Isabella. The large east window to the south aisle is of the Perpendicular period. On the south wall of the aisle is a window (figure 6) with Millennium glass and was dedicated during May 2000. The window was presented by the parishioners and the Parish Council and the work was carried out by Norfolk Stained Glass. Also in the aisle is a highly decorated piscina (figure 7).

Figure 8 shows the porch (also shown in figure 1). It was formerly single storey but during the 15th century an upper storey was added which was used as a Priest's Room. The staircase to this room is now closed. On the ground floor there are three windows on each side of the porch. Figure 9 is taken from the side of the porch so it shows the differences in the stonework from the original porch to the stonework when the upper floor was added.

Three flags hang in the church, a Union Jack, a flag of the Middlesex Regiment and a Regimental flag of the 65th General Hospital US Army. These flags commemorate not only parishioners who gave their lives during the last war, but those in the Middlesex Regiment and the US 65th General Hospital.

In the early days of the church, it was served by Monks from a nearby Priory but from 1305 to the present day there is a list of priests and rectors. Most of the present church (apart from the tower) is thought to have been built in the early 14th century in the Decorated style of architecture.

Figure 4

Figure 4a

Figure 5

Figure 6   *Figure 7*   *Figure 8*

St. Margaret's Church
Ilketshall, Suffolk

The church is set within a small village as shown in figure 1. It consists of a round west tower, nave, chancel and south porch which is shown more clearly in figure 2. The church is built with various flints sizes and some rough blocks of stone set in large amounts of mortar.

As with many of these churches, historians differ as to the actual date. Most historians date it no earlier than 12th century but some are convinced the tower up to the base of the belfry is Saxon probably just before 1000 AD and most of the church possibly of the same date.

In 1993 English Heritage decided to render the church tower. I understand this originally was white. I understand English Heritage offered to remove the rendering but the church decided to decline the offer because of cost. At the time of my visit the brightness

Figure 2

Figure 3

had softened and the tower is now more of a dirty beige. During the restoration two Saxon double splayed windows were discovered about 12 feet from the floor. These are shown clearly in figure 2 and in more detail in figure 3. The slit windows in the tower could be either Saxon or Norman. On entering the church through the south porch, which is possibly 16th/17th century, the first point of interest is the 15th century font with octagonal base with alternate decoration of blank shields and roses (figure 4). The bowl is supported by the pedestal with eight angel heads (figure 4a). The flat wooden decorated top is early 17th century. Four empty plinths around the base probably held four seated lions.

In the nave of the church (figure 5), pews and pulpit are Victorian. The chancel has a very distinctive roof (possibly timber) painted in very dark blue with gold stars. South of the chancel is the priest's door shown externally in figure 6 which clearly shows the ornamental panel above, possibly 18th century. Internally there is a small piscina (figure 7) also with a cusped ornamental head similar to that of the doorway (figure 6). The piscina is now close to floor as the sanctuary has been raised by the Victorians.

Figure 8 shows the east window, the glass is by Powell and Sons, circa 1860. The altar rails are Jacobean and are of high quality. The Royal Arms (figure 9) on the west wall (which are rather faint) are those of Queen Anne and are dated 1704.

Figure 4

The windows to the nave are 15th century but have been much restored. A round 19th century trefoil window has been added in the blocked north doorway.

Figure 4a

Figure 5

Figure 6

Figure 7

Figure 8

Figure 9

St. Peter's Church
Bruisyard, Suffolk

The church stands on rising ground overlooking the river Alde and is in a fairly isolated position except for four modern houses and a farm nearby. The church consists of a round west tower, nave, chancel, south transept and south porch (figure 1). The actual age of the church is uncertain but it is obviously very old and some historians think part may be Saxon. Figure 2 shows the tower in greater detail although the bulge in the tower can be seen more clearly in figure 1.

The tower is built of varying sized flints with some brick, possibly Tudor patchwork at lower nave roof level. The four double-light belfry windows are said to be possibly 14th century but restored mid-20th century. Local sources suggest that the tower was possibly a blockhouse for the Count of the Saxon Shore covering the ford in the River Alde below.

Figure 2

Figure 3

The nave is flint built, although there are patches of brick work again possibly Tudor, including the window shown in figure 3. A Nunnery was founded in Bruisyard in 1367 which was dissolved in 1542. Some of the materials used in the reign of Elizabeth I are thought to come from the demolished Nunnery.

The south transept is now used as a vestry and believed to have been built in the 16th century (built after the Dissolution of the Nunnery in 1542).

Near the entrance to the church is a 15th century font, very similar to others found in the Suffolk area. The bowl is decorated with plain shields and the shaft with seated lions (figure 4).

It is thought that two of the Duchesses of the House of Plantagenet who died in the Nunnery at Bruisyard lie buried beneath the nave floor although this is not certain as the only remains are the indents for the two small brasses. The simple but impressive pulpit is 18th century with a more modern lectern nearby (figure 5). Also in the nave is an unusual set of Royal Arms which is claimed locally to be possibly the 'worst executed in England'. It is painted on sacking with the arms of the House of Hanover and is dated approximately 1800 (figure 6).

Figure 7 shows the chancel with the east window, the stone reredos and the altar table believed to be Jacobean. In the south-east corner of the chancel can be seen a simple piscina in a niche.

Looking back from the chancel toward the tower (figure 8) can be seen the simple arched, braced roof. Figure 8 also shows the tower arch, the 15th century font, the pews and the west window in the tower. Figure 9 shows the town sign very close to the church which is self-explanatory.

Figure 4

Figure 5

Figure 6

Figure 7

Figure 8

Figure 9

All Saints Church
Ramsholt, Suffolk

This lovely old church, in the far south-eastern corner of Suffolk is in a beautiful raised position overlooking the Deben estuary. As well as being in a beautiful situation, it is also in an a very isolated position, being nearly a mile off the main road. It is said that a chart of 1287, in the reign of Edward III, shows the church as being a sea mark for vessels sailing on the Deben. It is even thought that this church, or possibly an earlier church at the same site, may have been used as a watch tower used by the Saxons against Viking invaders.

The existing church (figure 1) and church tower, shown more clearly in figure 2, are thought by most historians to be Norman and by some as even late Saxon. Other more modern historians feel it could be of a later period. The nave and chancel are rendered externally and parts may have been renovated at a later date.

Figure 2

The roof was certainly reroofed with tile and the outline of the original roof, thought to have been thatched, is shown in figure 2. The tower is quite unusual, thought by many to be oval but it appears to be actually round with three large, strong stone buttresses on the north, south and west sides giving the oval appearance. The church was built, particularly the tower, of undressed local stone comprising flint, brick and a local brown stone known as septaria, found on local beaches.

The lancet windows to the west of the tower are possibly Early English which may have influenced some historians that the tower was built at the same period. The tower arch, from the nave side, appears to be Norman although some historians say that the inside, on the tower side of the archway, there are signs of Saxon workmanship.

Figure 3

The entrance to the church is from the south-facing porch (figure 3), believed to be of 17th century brick. The actual doorway entrances on both the north and south side are said to be 13th century.

On entering the church, the first point of interest is the octagonal font (figure 4), the bowl is believed to be 15th century but with an earlier base, possibly Norman. The font has decoration of quatrefoil panels as shown more clearly in figure 4a.

Near the font there are two more interesting features, an ancient stone coffin (figure 5) which lies near the tower archway. Some historians feel that this may not have been an actual coffin, but a vessel to wash bodies before burial. On the south-western corner of the church is a wooden medieval chest (figure 6).

Figure 4

In the nave, the pews were intalled in 1857 with an unusual two-decker pulpit (figure 7) placed in the centre beside the south wall. Unusually, the pews to the east of the pulpit face inward toward the pulpit and not as usual, towards the altar table.

Figure 4a

The round headed windows on the south side are 13th and 14th century and those on the north side are 17th century and display several different styles. In the chancel, there is an early 14th century piscina with a dropped sedilia nearby to seat officiating clery (figure 8). The east window to the chancel is believed to be 13th century.

There have been many signs of refurbishment and restoration during the years. There was refurbishment in the 19th century with the new pews, etc., mentioned above and also restoration work in 1973/4 on the tower and the interior. The roof was altered as mentioned earlier.

Figure 5

Figure 6

Figure 7

Figure 8

Domesday Book References

The Domesday Book is divided into two sections, Great and Little Domesday, and all the information regarding Norfolk and Suffolk is in the Little Domesday section. The Domesday Book was initially known as the 'King's Book' or 'The Great Book of Winchester' where the Royal Treasury was based. The book was commissioned by William the Conqueror at Christmas 1085 and was completed by 1086/87 which must have been a mammoth job in view of the communication problems at the time, and it is quite possible that mistakes and omissions occurred quite innocently. During that period land changed hands fairly quickly and the book was said to be virtually out of date as soon as it had been compiled.

The main purpose of the book was to produce a record of the returns and resources of the land for the King's Treasury and it also shows the split between lands owned by the King and the various Lords, Bishops and Landowners who had been granted lands, estates and other property.

References to churches in the Domesday Book may be only partially complete as the main purpose of the book was to compile records to show returns to the King's Treasury. As I discovered, particularly during my investigations of North Norfolk churches, there were one or two churches in that area which were thought to date from 850/900 AD and yet were still not included in the Domesday Book.

For interest, I have listed the names of the villages showing their old English names as shown in the Domesday Book. For ease of reference, I have divided the churches between Norfolk and Suffolk and listed them in alphabetical order for each county.

Norfolk
Ashmanhough – not listed
Beachamwell (Beechamwell) – Becheswella; Bicham; Bycham; Hekeswella
Beeston St. Lawrence – Besetuna
Brampton – Brantuma
Brandiston – Brantestuna
Cockley Cley – Cleia
West Dereham – Derham; Dereham
Dilham – Dilham
Edingthorpe – not listed
Gayton Thorpe – Thorp; Torp
Lexham (East and West) – Leccesham; Lecesham
Taverham – Taverham
Tuttington – Tatituna; Tutincghetuna
Witton (Near North Walsham) – Widituna; Wittuna; Wituna
Worthing – not listed

Suffolk
Bruisyard – Buresiart
Ilketshall – Elcheteshala; Ilcheteleshala; Ilcheteshala
Ramsholt – Rammesholt
Rickingham Inferior – Richingehalla; Rikingahala
Risby – Resebi; Risebi; Riseby

Glossary

This book is written in an endeavour to raise interest in these churches and I have tried to keep the various details fairly simple but these additional notes maybe of assistance.

Aisle
These are extensions to the north and south sides of the nave.

Architectural Styles (approximate dates)
Saxon –	*7th Century to 1066*
Norman –	*1066 to approximately 1200*
Transititional –	*A period between Norman and Early English periods from approximately 1150 to 1200*
Early English –	*1200 to approximately 1300 including lancet and early tracery styles*
Decorated –	*1300 to approximation 1350 includes 'Y' tracery and reticulated style*
Perpendicular –	*From approximately 1400. This includes the Tudor styling and a Jacobean period of 1603 to 1625 during the reign of James I.*
Gothic –	*Covers an 'overall' period from approximately 1200 to 1500*

Bier
A moveable frame on which a coffin or a corpse is carried.

Black Death
1349–50 – killed 20–30% of the national population but possibly over a half of the population of Norfolk.

Carstone
Also known as gingerbread stone because of its reddish brown colour (caused by iron ore particles). Very much a north-west Norfolk stone.

Chancel
Eastern part of the church, housing the main altar and usually the choir.

Clerestory
This is an upper row of windows in a large church, above the level of the aisle roofs.

Conglomerate
Also known as pudding stone. Normally a harder stone than carstone and usually contains pebbles in its structure. It was originally found in the surface soil and mainly used pre-Conquest.

Corbels
These are supports, usually stone, projecting from a wall to carry the weight of the roof timbers. These are often decorated with decorative heads.

Hatchments
The Arms of a deceased person set on a black lozenge-shaped background. These hatchments were often placed in front of the home of the deceased before burial and then transferred to the church.

Lancet
Narrow, tall, acutely arched windows.

Nave
The main body of the church

Piscina
This is a sink or stone basin usually near the altar in pre-Reformation churches for draining water used during a mass or communion. The water being drained into the consecrated foundations of the church.

Reformation
1534 when Henry VIII broke away from the Church of Rome and established the Protestant Church of England.

Reredos
An ornamental screen covering the wall at the back of the altar.

Rood Screen
A screen used to divide the chancel from the nave in many churches. In medieval churches these were largely damaged at the time of the Reformation.

Royal Coat of Arms
These were introduced into many churches after the Reformation when Henry VIII became Supreme Head of the Church of England 1534.

Sedilia
Stone seats or set of seats in the wall of medieval churches in the chancel usually near the piscina. This is where priests sat during long services.

Stoup
Usually a small stone bowl for holy water in the porches of many early churches, the water being used for parishioners to bless themselves.

Tracery
Ornate stone ribs in the upper part of windows, also seen in circular windows.

Transept
Extensions to the north and south body of the church, often leaving the church with a plan shape of the cross.

Bibliography and Suggested Additional Reading

I would like to acknowledge my thanks to the authors of some of the books listed below that have helped me in my introduction to round tower churches. If you have found the subject of round tower churches interesting, I would recommend you consider reading some these additional books:

Norfolk Churches Great and Small by C.V. Roberts and Richard Tilbrook – an excellent book with many magnificent photographs and interesting information.

Suffolk Churches Great and Small by Roy Tricker, George Pipe and Richard Tilbrook – another first class book in a similar style to *Norfolk Churches Great and Small* as above.

The Popular Guide to Norfolk Churches by T.D. Mortlock and C.V. Roberts – a series of books containing detailed information on Norfolk churches.

Round Towered Churches of South East England by W.J. Goode – a virtual wealth of information. A great result for over 30 years endeavour.

The Round Towered Churches of Norfolk by Dorothy Shreeve and Lynn Stillgoe – a book of wonderful illustrations.

England's 1,000 Best Churches by Simon Jenkins. The contents of this book were a feature of a Channel 4 television series a couple of years ago. This book covers a selection of England's finest churches and includes four of the churches visited in my suggested tours – namely Hadiscoe and Hales in Norfolk and Barsham and Bramfield in Suffolk.

The Round Tower Church Towers of England by Stephen Hart – a detailed architectural study of round church towers in England is of great interest to those wishing to study the architecture in greater detail.

The Buildings of England – Norfolk and Suffolk Editions by Nikolaus Pevsner – these very detailed books covering all counties of Britain, were started in the 20th century with many revisions and editions since. These books detail not only churches but all important buildings.

Miscellaneous church booklets – I would particularly mention a booklet entitled 'The Parish Churches of the Hempnall Group', covering all eight churches in the group – not all are round tower.

If your interest in round tower churches has been roused, why not consider joining The Round Tower Churches Society. Details of membership can be found in many churches. If you do decide to join, you will receive quarterly copies of their very interesting magazine containing analysis of specific Round Tower Churches and comments on many others. Also The Round Tower Churches Society arranges tours to visit various groups of churches.